Wildflowers

William Reynolds

of Canada

Wildflowers
of Canada

William Reynolds

B. Mitchell

Produced by Discovery Books for:
B. Mitchell
98 Carrier Drive
Rexdale, Ontario
M9W 5R1
ISBN: 0-99994-398-7

Printed and bound in Hong Kong
88 89 90 2 3 4 5

Acknowledgements

I wish to thank the following people for their encouragement, assistance and advice: Roger Boulton, John Duff, Margaret Fleming Reynolds and Marion Reynolds.

Special thanks must be given to Ted Dyke, Paul and Terry Pratt, and Helene Danner for permission to reproduce their photographs. I wish to thank Helene Danner also for her efforts in typing the manuscript of this book.

W.R.

Photo credits: Helene Danner, 126   Ted Dyke, 90
Paul and Terry Pratt, 41, 44, 46, 65, 74, 77
All other photographs are by the author.

Page 1: Smooth rose *(Rosa blanda)*

Named for its thornless stem, this beautiful native rose is one of many species to be found in North America. Other members of the rose family include apple, cherry and peach trees, as well as the prickly rose (Rosa acicularis).

Page 2: Trumpet creeper *(Campsis radicans)*

This woody vine with its large, colorful trumpet-like flowers is often visited by nectar-seeking hummingbirds. Blossoming in midsummer, the trumpet creeper inhabits the open woodland and low thicket areas of Illinois, Michigan and New Jersey south to Florida. It may also be seen in rare Canadian environments.

Contents

Wet grassland habitat

Introduction

Wildflowers can be found growing in all but the most inhospitable terrain. In North America, a myriad of environments large and small await the wildflower enthusiast—sun-scorched deserts and cool woodland ponds, watery bogs and mountain slopes. Each provides a habitat for thousands of species that grow in a wondrous array of color and aroma, shape and texture.

Plants, like all living organisms, have evolved over the millenia to meet the specific environmental dictates of the habitat to which they belong. Many organic, geological and atmospheric variables, such as the acidity or alkalinity of the soils and water, the duration and intensity of sunlight and the elevation of the landmass are critical factors that define a habitat and the nature of the numerous species of wildflower found within it.

Flourishing in nitrogen-poor sphagnum bogs, the carnivorous northern pitcher plant (*Sarracenia purpurea*—page 90) is a fascinating species and one truly suited to its environment. Unable to obtain adequate nutrients solely from the surrounding soils and water, this species, like its relative Florida's common hooded pitcher plant (*Sarracenia minor*), supplements its diet by the passive digestion of insects that enter and drown in the water-filled pitchers.

Sharing the pitcher plant's boggy habitat, the thread-leaved sundew (*Drosera filiformis*—page 101) and others of the sundew family are endowed with glistening droplets of a sticky liquid with which they trap unsuspecting insects. By consuming the ensnared insects, sundews, too, are able to supplement their meager diet.

The prickly pear cactus (*Opuntia compressa*—page 18) may be found in the arid, desert-like soil conditions of some unique eastern environments, such as a tiny enclave in southwestern Ontario and in specific locales in Massachusetts and Minnesota as well as in its primary habitat, the arid zones of western North America. Like the beavertail cactus (*Opuntia basilaris*) of the famous Mojave Desert and the showy hedgehog cactus (*Echinocerus* sp.—page 46) of Texas, the prickly pear is particularly well-suited to a demanding environment. Shallow root systems spread out laterally from the plant's communal clusters allowing the species to absorb quickly and subsequently benefit from whatever moisture becomes available.

In both desert and desert-like habitats, the few resilient green plants that do exist are tempting sources of food for the resident mammalian herbivores. The needle-sharp spines of the prickly pear, however, prohibit such foraging activity. In fact, the dense spines have taken the place of leaves, for leaves of any description allow varying amounts of water vapor to be lost to the atmosphere. The broad, flattened, pad-like green stems of the cactus are, in reality, succulent reservoirs employed by the plant to cope with its environment.

Apart from these obvious adaptations of the prickly pear cactus, the most wonderful aspect of this flower's existence for many people is the plant's very presence in eastern environments. It appears in locales which seldom suggest that desert-like conditions prevail or that plant types most commonly associated with true deserts may be found here. The prickly pear flourishes in the east in isolated pockets where the environmental conditions reflect, or at least partially mimic the larger western arid environments.

Quite unlike the prickly pear, both in its favored environment and its design, the diminutive round-lobed hepatica (*Hepatica americana* — page 54) is a communal wildflower of the temperate forests. This species must regularly contend with the maiming frost and bitter winds that still prevail in early spring. To cope with such life-threatening conditions, this hardy plant has developed defense mechanisms suitable to the rigorous challenges of its early blossoming. Each delicate stem is covered by a dense mass of protective hairs that acts as an insulator, shielding the new shoots from the frigid air that continues to linger in winter's wake. In a similar environment, the bloodroot (*Sanguinaria canadensis* — pages 42–43) must contend with these same conditions. To accomplish this task, the verdant, broad leaves of this species cowl about the frail, budding

blossom. Thus sheltered, the flower survives and the plant's continued existence is ensured.

Both species are heliotropic; their blossoms follow the course of the moving sun. Cupped like tiny parabolic reflectors, each flower generates warmth and, amazingly, the center of each bloom is several degrees warmer than the plant's surrounding environment. The earliest insects are attracted to the warmth found in the flowers and assist in the pollination of both species. The tiny, frail blossoms of these two harbingers of spring are visible only by day, however, for they close as daylight fades and the chill evening air descends upon the forest.

Travelling throughout the United States and Canada, one is able to appreciate the forces of earth's geological and atmospheric changes that have created its awe-inspiring features — towering, wind-scoured mountain ranges, grass-covered prairies, arid deserts and steep-walled canyons. Each of these environments provides a habitat for a wide variety of beautifully-adapted wildflowers. Like the animal populations about them, these plants have had to cope with the changing rhythms and often cataclysmic events of the natural world. Each environment places its own demands on living things and wildflowers have had to acclimatize to them no less than other plant and animal species.

Many visible physical characteristics of wildflowers assist us in understanding the environmental factors affecting them. Tall, slender-stemmed, broad-leaved plants and squat, hairy or leafless varieties are obviously dissimilar, and it is these dissimilarities that provide us with information concerning habitat and climate conditions. Constant extremes in temperature, drought or high levels of precipitation, soil types, wind and differing elevations of the land-mass can all contribute to a plant's size, shape and, even, color.

Broad-leaved species, such as the marsh marigold (*Caltha palustris* — page 52) can absorb enormous quantities of water and nutrients into the plant via the root system. The leaves, however, suggest that this species has little need of storing any significant quantity of water in reserve, since such leaf structures allow the plant to emit large volumes of water vapor into the atmosphere, a process known as transpiration. Large-surfaced leaf design suggests a relatively warm, moist environment with an abundance of water or, in other words, a temperate climate. The southern deciduous forests, dominated by broad-leaved species, release significantly higher levels of water vapor into the atmosphere than do the northern, or boreal, coniferous forests. The tropical rain forest, as an example, is dominated by large, broad-leaved species which create so much water vapor that the forest releases into the atmosphere much of the water that will return as the jungle's heavy rain.

In contrast, plants of much cooler and dryer regions, such as the boreal conifers, have developed tough, needle-like leaves that allow far less water vapor to escape. To appreciate the physical dissimilarities between the temperate zone species of plant life and the arctic or boreal species, we need not travel hundreds or thousands of miles north to an arctic environment. Instead, we can simply change our elevation. As we ascend from temperate zones and a more or less uniform deciduous forest, we begin to observe a changing forest community. Eventually, we reach elevations dominated by conif-

erous trees and generally shorter, narrower-leaved wildflowers. Ascending further, we pass the treeline and enter a wind-swept realm of rocky crags and pinnacles that exhibit many of the same kinds of dwarf floral adaptations as are found in the arctic regions.

In both the alpine and arctic habitats, two topographically dissimilar environments, many of the same seasonal, life-threatening conditions prevail. Ravaged for much of the year by bitter, desiccating winds, both terrains perpetually offer severe challenges to the survival of plants and animals. Because of this, the resident wild-flower population is a predominantly ground-hugging assemblage of species that are resilient enough to survive under these inhospitable conditions. Tenaciously clinging to life, these plants of the northern tundra and the mountainous elevations of the south are small in comparison with species found in more temperate regions. The life-sustaining warmth radiating from the earth's surface is quickly swept away as it rises. What meager benefits of warmth the sun's rays bestow are found nearest the earth itself. Therefore, to remain sheltered from the chilling blasts of wind that frequent its northern and alpine domains, the tiny purple saxifrage (*Saxifraga oppositi-folia* — page 44) grows to a height of only four inches.

Through an understanding of the critical, interdependent relationships established among all living things, we are best able to realize the importance and the intrinsic value of wildflowers. We can begin to enjoy these beautiful flowers not just because they are aesthetically pleasing, but also because they are integral parts of a much larger and more intriguing whole — the plant's habitat and its place in the biosphere.

Spring

Page 11: Common blue violet (Viola papilionacea)

Flourishing in clusters in damp meadows and forests, this native violet occasionally may be found rimmed with silver frost on a spring morning. This eight-inch-high plant, and many other native violets such as the long-spurred violet (Viola rostrata), appear throughout a wide range in North America.

Left:
Fringed polygala, gaywings
(*Polygala paucifolia*)

This exotic-looking species is a dazzling inhabitant of the spring woodland throughout much of northern Illinois, New England and eastern Canada. Often incorrectly identified as an orchid by the beginning naturalist, these delicate blossoms grow in groups close to the ground. Each flower appears above the rich, moist soil and has developed from a hidden, buried weave of stems.

Right:
Pussy willow
(*Salix discolor*)

The furry flowers of the pussy willow are, for many people, the first, long-awaited signal of spring. In response, many venture out to favorite, moist thickets and streambanks to collect stems of the blossoms for bouquets.

Left: False Solomon's-seal (*Smilacina racemosa*)

Known in the Pacific states as branched Solomon's-seal, this three-foot-high species appears over a wide range in North America. True Solomon's-seals, such as the smooth Solomon's-seal (Polygonatum biflorum) bear their pendant, bell-like blossoms along the underside of the leafy stem, unlike the upright flowers of false Solomon's-seal.

Above: Bullhead lily (*Nuphar variegatum*)

A member of the water lily family, this species is related to the famous lotus of ancient mythology. It grows widely in North America and its distinctive shape and color are a common sight on bogland pools and other still waters.

Left:
Labrador tea
(*Ledum groenlandicum*)

A member of the heath family, the leaves of this hardy species were once used to make tea. Favoring cold, acidic bogs, this boreal shrub may be found from Greenland and Labrador south to Washington and west to Alberta.

Right:
Jack-in-the-pulpit,
Indian turnip
(*Arisaema atrorubens*)

*Inhabiting the damp recesses of deciduous woodlands and streambanks, this spring wildflower appears singly or in loose-knit communities throughout much of eastern North America from Quebec to Florida. Reaching a height of two feet, this species is related to wild calla (*Calla palustris*). The taproot was once cooked and eaten by native peoples, hence the name Indian turnip. It is, however, dangerous if eaten raw.*

Left: Prickly pear cactus (*Opuntia compressa*)

These waxy, yellow three inch blossoms flourish in the desert spring and are a common sight in the arid environments of western North America. This species is also the only cactus to grow in the isolated pockets of the eastern United States and southern Ontario that boast a desert-like habitat.

Above: Common strawberry (*Fragaria virginiana*)

The common, or wild, strawberry grows in open, sunny areas throughout most of North America. The plant grows near to the ground, producing small, white blossoms from April to June and berries in June and July. Wild strawberries have a stronger, deeper flavor than the domesticated varieties.

Above: Purple-flowering raspberry (*Rubus odoratus*)

The genus name Rubus refers to the reddish fruits borne by this species and others like the thimbleberry (Rubus parviflorus). Unfortunately, the fruit of the purple-flowering raspberry is dry, markedly acidic and unpleasant to eat. A member of the rose family, this species frequents many dry, sandy or rock-strewn terrains, thickets and roadsides, from Quebec to Georgia and Tennessee.

Right: Long-spurred violet (*Viola rostrata*)

One of the most striking of the many native violets, this beautiful, long-spurred flower of the moist forests of spring may be found throughout much of southern Ontario and Quebec and south into the uplands of West Virginia and Alabama.

Left: Canada anemone (*Anemone canadensis*)

The Canada anemone inhabits an enormous range from Labrador and Alberta as far south as New Mexico. Massive groups of this species may be seen in late spring in moist meadows and on slopes. What appear to be white petals are, in this instance, showy sepals.

Above: Golden ragwort (*Senecio aureus*)

Numerous ragworts may be found throughout eastern and midwestern North America. Reaching a height of two feet, this species appears singly or in small groups in the wet meadows and woodlands of early spring.

Showy orchis
(*Galearis spectabilis*)

One of the dozens of North American orchids, this small, hooded flower often goes unnoticed among the jumble of lush spring undergrowth and the fallen trees of moist woodlands and swamps. Reaching a height of from five to twelve inches, this orchid is, like many members of its family, extremely susceptible to destruction by the careless human visitor. Even tiny changes in the habitat can signal the demise of this elegant, fragrant flower.

Blue flag, wild blue iris
(*Iris versicolor*)

This exotic, native flower is one of approximately fifteen hundred species of plants that constitute the iris family. Each plant reaches a height of three feet and large stands of blue flag may be seen in wet meadows and at the edges of streams and lakes.

Yellow lady's slipper
(*Cypripedium calceolus*)

Few sights in nature are as exquisite as a leafy stand of these showy native orchids. Photographed on a rainy morning in June, these waxy blossoms seemed to glow in their moist woodland home. Reaching a height of twenty-eight inches, each stem bears a fragile two-inch waxy slipper.

Above: Painted trillium (*Trillium undulatum*)

Found throughout much of Manitoba, Ontario, eastern Quebec, Wisconsin, Pennsylvania and northern New Jersey, the painted trillium grows in acidic, cool woodlands and, sometimes, bogs. The vibrant crimson of the heart of each wavy petal is unique among trilliums. Appearing singly or in groups, this delicate lily may reach a height of nearly twenty inches. Short-lived and easily damaged, this species, like other wildflowers, should not be picked.

Right: Red trillium (*Trillium erectum*)

Beautiful but malodorous, the red trillium frequents the cool, rich woodlands of Delaware, Pennsylvania, Quebec and Ontario. Its foul aroma, while unpleasant to the human nose, attracts carrion flies, one of the flower's primary pollinators.

Above: Mossy stonecrop (*Sedum acre*)

A native European species, this diminutive, succulent herb favors dry, rock-strewn terrain. It is related to several western species including lanceleaf sedum (Sedum lanceolatum) of the Pacific United States. Of the approximately fifteen hundred family members found worldwide, some, such as the jade tree, have become common household plants.

Right: Early saxifrage (*Saxifraga virginiensis*)

A relative of the dainty, white-petalled brook saxifrage (Saxifraga punctata) of the Pacific states, this species appears in early spring. Reaching a maximum height of sixteen inches, large, communal masses of early saxifrage may often be found in the dry, rocky terrain of eastern North America. There are more than five hundred species of saxifrage, most of which are found in the northern hemisphere.

Coltsfoot
(*Tussilago farfara*)

Groups of this introduced species appear in early spring along the gravel edges of roads and open waste places. A native of Eurasia, the plant has a long history of human use. Its large leaves, which appear only after the blossoms and stems have died away, were once dried and used for tea. The leaves were also employed in the preparation of a cough syrup.

Downy yellow violet
(*Viola pubescens*)

This cheerful, delicate violet is found in the same spring woodland habitat as the common blue violet (Viola papilionacea). Its petals are bright yellow with the lower ones being brownish- or purplish-veined. The entire plant is covered with soft, downy hairs.

Wild lily-of-the-valley
(*Maianthemum canadense*)

Also referred to as the Canada mayflower, this diminutive woodland species forms lush, green mats in its moist spring habitat. Each individual blossom within the cluster measures only one-sixth of an inch.

Great white trillium
(*Trillium grandiflorum*)

The largest of the native trilliums, this flower appears in clusters in the rich, moist woodlands of spring. Reaching a height of eighteen inches, it may be seen in Ontario, Quebec and south to Maine, Georgia and Arkansas.

Herb Robert
(*Geranium robertianum*)

Common to Europe and parts of North America including New England, Ohio, Indiana, Ontario, Manitoba and Quebec, this tiny geranium frequents the cool shade of rocky woodlands and quiet ravines. Legend attributes the name of this small, lavender flower to Robert Goodfellow, the famous Robin Hood.

Left:
Bunchberry
(*Cornus canadensis*)

Dense carpets of this small woodland dogwood are not uncommon. Bunchberry and its much larger relative, the Pacific dogwood (Cornus nuttallii) may be seen in British Columbia and California. The cream-colored "blossoms" of both species are merely showy sepals surrounding the much tinier, true flowers in the center.

Right:
Wild columbine
(*Aquilegia canadensis*)

The name columbine is derived from French and Latin, meaning "dove-like," a reference to the petals' resemblance to five passively-perched doves. This woodland species is a member of the buttercup family and flowers in rocky, sun-washed areas in spring.

Large-flowered bellwort
(*Uvularia grandiflora*)

*Large numbers of this wood-
land species appear in
spring throughout much of
eastern North America.
Reaching a height of twenty
inches, the plant's pendant
flowers hang like an uvula
or soft palate, hence the
name* uvularia.

Small white lady's slipper
(*Cypripedium candidum*)

This delicate orchid may be found in Ontario, Manitoba south into Michigan, and Missouri. A western species, (Cypripedium montanum), may be found in the mountainous regions of the United States. Unfortunately, the small white lady's slipper is now considered both rare and endangered in parts of its range.

Bloodroot
(*Sanguinaria canadensis*)

A communal flower of early spring, this plant can appear in enormous masses along the edges of streams or in the moist, leaf-littered woodlands of most of northeastern and northcentral North America. When damaged, the stems of this plant exude a red juice from which the common name is derived. This same crimson liquid was once used by pioneers and native peoples as a dye.

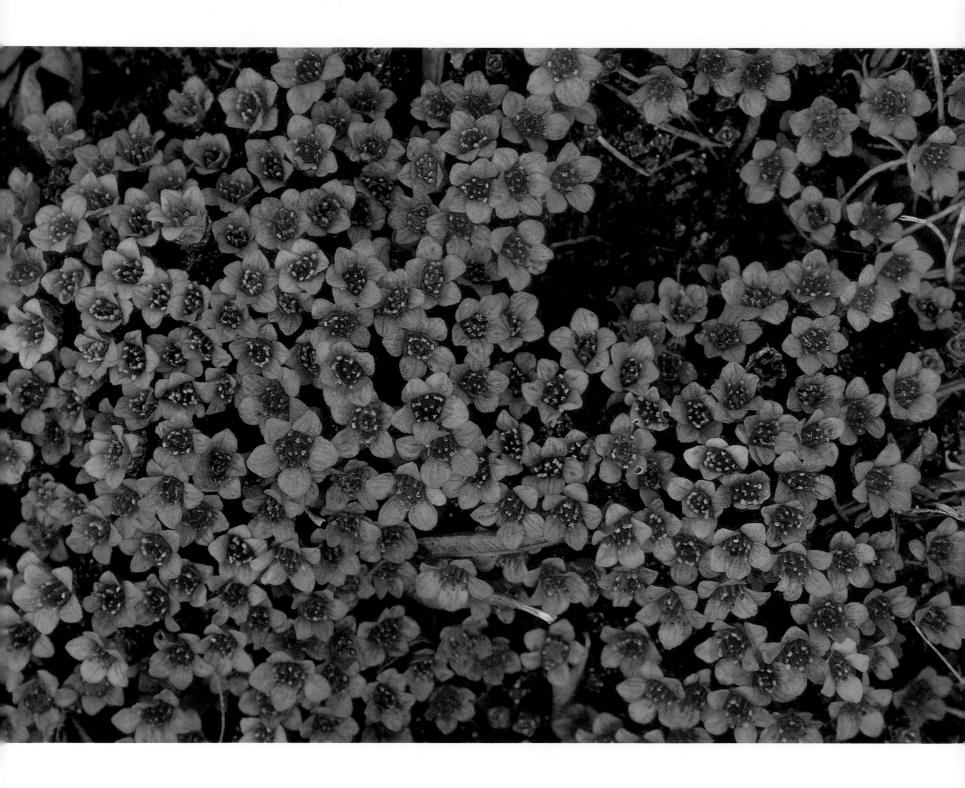

Left: Purple saxifrage (*Saxifraga oppositifolia*)

Alpine and arctic terrains are the habitat of these Lilliputian flowers that are so well-adapted to the bitterly cold air and savage winds of mountainous regions and the arctic tundra. This showy species can be found on the rocky cliffs and seemingly lifeless ledges of the mountains of British Columbia, Washington and Wyoming, in northern Vermont, Newfoundland and Quebec, and in the far north.

Above: Dutchman's breeches (*Dicentra cucullaria*)

Appearing in clusters in the cool, moist woodland soils of spring, this fragrant plant is aptly named, for it looks like tiny clotheslines of airing breeches. A member of the poppy family, this twelve-inch-high native species may be found in Quebec and Ontario, Alabama, eastern Kansas and in mountainous regions south to Georgia.

Left:
Hedgehog cactus
(*Echinocerus* sp.)

The beautiful hedgehog cactus is one of many species of desert plants that may be seen throughout much of the southern United States. Related to the prickly pear cactus (Opuntia compressa), the hedgehog cactus has developed specific, physical adaptations designed to meet the rigorous challenges of its harsh environment. Shallow roots aid in capturing the water of infrequent rainfall, and the needle-sharp spines serve to deter animals from browsing on the plant.

Right:
Wild ginger
(*Asarum canadense*)

A unique inhabitant of spring woodlands, this communal flower is first located by its showy, broad leaves that appear as verdant, irregular mats on the forest floor. The tri-lobed blossoms often remain hidden below the brown leaf litter of the previous autumn. The plant's root has an aroma similar to that of ginger.

46

Clintonia, bluebead lily
(*Clintonia borealis*)

A predominantly communal species, this bell-flowered lily may be found in the moist, cool, acidic woodlands of much of Labrador, Quebec and Ontario. Rising from two shiny, basal leaves, the stem bearing the yellowish-green blossoms may reach a height of fifteen inches. The flowers are later replaced by the rich blue berries that give the plant one of its common names.

Trout-lily
(*Erythronium americanum*)

A woodland species, this colorful member of the lily family may carpet the forest floor with clusters of bobbing yellow flowers. Before flowering, the mottled basal leaves most readily identify this harbinger of spring. Reaching a height of from four to ten inches, this small lily is but one of an estimated four to six thousand species of lily appearing throughout the world. Some of these are poisonous; others, like the onion, are a common table food.

Foamflower
(*Tiarella cordifolia*)

*A relative of purple saxi-
frage (*Saxifraga oppositifolia),
*this communal, native wild-
flower appears in rich
woodland soil in spring and
early summer. Large colo-
nies of finely-textured, tiny
white flowers grow in the
forest shade, and resemble
the seafoam that gives them
their common name.*

Left:
Marsh marigold, cowslip
(*Caltha palustris*)

This spring wildflower appears in enormous numbers, populating marshes and wet meadows with its yellow blooms. In Europe, where it is commonly referred to as kingcup, this species was once used to lend color to butter.

Right:
Canada violet
(*Viola canadensis*)

A relative of the pansy, this native woodland species appears throughout much of southern Canada and south into mountainous regions of the eastern and midwestern United States. To assist identification of violets, it is valuable to note that some species are "stemmed"—bearing both leaves and blossoms on the same stalk. Other violets are "stemless"—the leaves and flowers being borne by separate stalks. This species is a stemmed variety.

Above: Round-lobed hepatica (*Hepatica americana*)

*Related to the sharp-lobed hepatica (*Hepatica acutiloba*), this clustering flower of early spring appears in woodland habitats throughout much of southern Canada and south into areas such as Alabama, Minnesota and northern Florida. Reaching a height of six inches, each hairy stem bears a small blossom that opens and closes each day.*

Right: Barren strawberry (*Waldsteinia fragarioides*)

*This diminutive, communal species blossoms in late spring and early summer. A member of the rose family, it is related to both the purple-flowering raspberry (*Rubus odoratus*) and common strawberry (*Fragaria virginiana*). Unlike the common strawberry, however, the fruit of the barren strawberry is inedible.*

Goldthread, canker-root
(*Coptis trifolia* ssp.
groenlandica)

*The golden-yellow, thread-
like subterranean stems of
this one-half-inch flower
were once used by native
peoples and pioneer settlers
to treat canker sores of the
mouth. Growing in moist
coniferous woodlands and
the shaded periphery of
swamps, these small blos-
soms range from Greenland
to the mountains of North
Carolina and west to Iowa.*

Partridgeberry
(Mitchella repens)

Found throughout most of central and eastern North America, this low, trailing, woodland creeper often carpets the forest floor with its evergreen leaves. The tiny, fragrant blossoms appear in late spring and early summer and are eventually replaced by glistening red berries.

Left: Sharp-lobed hepatica (*Hepatica acutiloba*)

This hepatica appears well before the spring woodland canopy of leaves arrives. It is able to flourish in abundant sunlight in the dry, sometimes rocky, deciduous forests of Manitoba and Ontario south to Alabama, Georgia and Missouri.

Above: Fragrant white water lily (*Nymphaea odorata*)

Floating on still ponds against the dark green background of their lily pads, these beautiful white flowers spread their perfume on the morning air of late spring and summer. The large, buried stems of this lily are eaten by muskrats, while its pads are a frequent resting place for dragonflies and frogs.

Summer

Page 61:
Wood lily
(*Lilium philadelphicum*)

Splashes of red in the dry prairies and woodlands of summer often signal the presence of this native lily. Appearing singly or in groups, this showy species reaches a height of three feet, and may be found from British Columbia to Quebec and south into the eastern United States. The fleshy bulbs of this hardy plant were often used by native people for food.

Left:

Viper's bugloss, blueweed
(*Echium vulgare*)

Introduced from Europe, this communal plant has since spread throughout much of the northeastern United States and southern Canada. Preferring dry waste sites, road edges and fields, large masses of this two-foot species are a common sight in midsummer. Once established in an area, the plant can become prolific, causing some to regard the species as an obnoxious, albeit beautiful, pest.

Culver's root
(*Veronicastrum virginicum*)

*The tall, stately spikes of
this six-foot midsummer
plant appear in the moist
meadows and open wood-
lands of Vermont, Louisiana,
northwestern Florida, Manitoba and elsewhere. Each
tiny blossom in the cluster
measures one quarter of an
inch.*

Paintbrush
(*Castilleja* sp.)

There are approximately two hundred species of paintbrush found in the western hemisphere. Different habitats can engender distinctly different species. The desert paintbrush (Castilleja sp.), right, is found in the arid regions of the American southwest. Indian paintbrush (Castilleja coccinea), left, is by far the most common and can be found throughout North America.

Left: Woodland sunflower (*Helianthus divaricatus*)

In late summer, groups of this stately seven-foot plant can be seen in many woodland habitats. Appearing from Quebec, Ontario and Saskatchewan south to North Dakota and Georgia, this native species has many relatives in North America including the lance-leaved coreopsis (Coreopsis lanceolata) and the bull thistle (Cirsium vulgare).

Above: Wrinkled rose (*Rosa rugosa*)

One of many non-native wildflowers that now appear in North America, this plant originated in the Orient. Tall and heavily spined, this species bears large, three-inch wrinkled blossoms.

Left:
Yellow goatsbeard
(*Tragopogon pratensis*)

*Both the yellow goatsbeard and its purple-petalled relative, the oyster plant or salsify (*Tragopogon porrifolius*), were introduced to this continent by early settlers from Europe who harvested the roots of both species for food. Today, these three-foot-high plants may be found throughout much of the United States and southern Canada.*

Right:
Low bindweed
(*Convolvulus spithamaeus*)

A member of the morning glory family, this short, trailing inhabitant of dry, sandy areas and rocky soils grows widely in eastern North America.

Butterfly-weed (*Asclepias tuberosa*)

Photographs of this milkweed seldom capture the vibrant orange of these tiny, clustered flowers. Common to dry, open fields and prairies as far south as Texas, Florida and Arizona, this plant is aptly named for the wandering butterflies that visit it in search of food. Milkweeds, of which there are about two thousand species, usually produce a thick milk-white juice from the stalk or stem when damaged. However, this species produces none of the milky substance. While distributed widely in a variety of habitats, most members of this family of plants appear in tropical regions.

Chicory, blue sailors
(*Cichorium intybus*)

A native species of Europe and Asia later introduced to North America, this mid-summer plant inhabits dry, open ditches, fields and the borders of roadways. The root of this plant is harvested, roasted, ground and used as a substitute for coffee.

Common foxglove
(*Digitalis purpurea*)

*A native of Europe, this spe-
cies now appears across
much of Canada and in
many regions of the United
States. Frequenting the dry
soils of road edges and open
fields, the tall, swaying
masses of pink-purple bells
make a lovely addition to
these summer habitats.*

Left: White-fringed orchid (*Platanthera blephariglottis*)

Another of the native orchids, and certainly one of the showiest species, this exotic plant flowers in marshes, sphagnum bogs and moist meadows. It is found in southern Quebec, Newfoundland south to Florida, through the Gulf coast and Mississippi.

Above: Gray-headed coneflower (*Ratibida pinnata*)

Rhythmically swaying in the warm summer breezes, this elegant five-foot plant frequents dry woods and grasslands in southern Ontario, Georgia and Oklahoma. One of many indigenous species of sunflower, it is related to the California coneflower (Rudbeckia californica) that can be found in the mountain meadows of the western United States.

Indian pipe
(*Monotropa uniflora*)

A parasitic species, Indian pipe is most commonly found flowering amid the moist woodland jumble of fallen tree limbs and decaying leaves. Its food source is a fungus that inhabits the humus of the forest floor.

Fringed gentian
(*Gentianella crinita*)

Open meadows would never be the same without this beautiful flower. In some parts of its range, this species, like too many others, has been placed on the rare and endangered list due mainly to overpicking. Found from southern Yukon to British Columbia, east to Quebec and south to Maine, Georgia and Montana, few blues in nature's realm can equal that of these delicate gentians.

Left:
Common mullein
(*Verbascum thapsus*)

An introduced species, this unique biennial has a long history of human use. It was once employed to create hair dye, herbal medicines and was even used as insulation in pioneer footwear. Reaching a height of up to six feet, this plant appears in dry fields and waste places throughout much of the United States and Canada.

Right:
Black-eyed Susan
(*Rudbeckia hirta*)

A member of the composite family of flowers, this showy and common inhabitant of open fields and roadsides often grows in large masses that look like dazzling wind-blown seas of yellow. This native plant most likely originated in the broad fertile expanse of the Great Plains. Today it may be seen throughout much of North America.

Above: Bunchberry (fruit) (*Cornus canadensis*)

The brilliant red berries of this dwarf dogwood fruit from late July to October and are more familiar to many people than the white blossoms of spring. The bunchberry is a favorite food for many birds but is inedible for humans.

Right: Virgin's bower (*Clematis virginiana*)

It is not uncommon to see this climbing vine draped over and around old fencelines or at the edge of moist thickets. Occasionally, too, these densely-packed flowers trail out over the ground like a flowing tumble of water. A member of the buttercup family, this summer species is related to the marsh marigold (Caltha palustris).

Left:
Red baneberry
(*Actaea rubra*)

*The round, clustered white blossoms of this species are replaced in late summer by the glistening, red berries for which the plant is named. Like its relative, the white baneberry (*Actaea pachypoda), *the fruit is beautiful but very poisonous.*

Right:
Slender ladies' tresses
(*Spiranthes gracilis*)

One of our most delicate and beautiful native orchids, this slender spindle of blossoms is appropriately named for its chain of minute blossoms. Unlike many of its relatives, this species survives in dry, sandy soil environments. It reaches a height of two feet, each frail stem bearing tiny flowers that move with the slightest breath of air.

Small purple-fringed orchis
(*Platanthera psycodes*)

Amazingly, many North Americans continue to associate orchids with distant cultures, exotic lands and tropical climates. Yet this spectacular summer orchid, with its clustered raceme of delicate, feathery blossoms appears throughout a large area of our continent. These beautiful plants are so fragile and their habitats are so delicately balanced that many species of orchid are endangered or rare because of human carelessness and wilful abuse.

Prairie loosestrife
(*Lysimachia quadriflora*)

Lovely, individual bouquets and small communities of this summer flower are commonly observed in the moist soils and prairie habitats of Manitoba, southern Ontario and western New York south to Missouri and Kentucky.

Hairy beardtongue
(*Penstemon hirsutus*)

In open woodlands and other dry areas in early summer, the hairy beardtongue grows in profusion. Its delicate, tubular flowers are blue or purplish at the base with white lobes. The stems and leaves are hairy and often sticky, giving the plant its common name.

Above: Northern pitcher plant (*Sarracenia purpurea*)

This unique inhabitant of sphagnum bogs is a carnivorous plant. It supplements its diet by the digestion of insects that become trapped in the plant's "pitchers." Several other species of pitcher plant may be found in North America including the California pitcher plant (Darlingtonia californica) and the trumpet (Sarracenia flava).

Right: Virginia mountain mint (*Pycnanthemum virginianum*)

Enormous, communal masses of this tiny-blossomed species appear in midsummer. A relative of wild bergamot (Monarda fistulosa), this plant may be found in dry fields and thickets from southwestern Ontario to Ohio, Maine and Missouri.

Left: Slender bush-clover (*Lespedeza virginica*)

Flowering in midsummer, the tiny blossoms quickly identify this plant as a member of the pea family. Each flower in the dense cluster measures only one-quarter of an inch. Like many of its relatives, this species inhabits dry soils and open clearings.

Above: Swamp milkweed (*Asclepias incarnata*)

Related to the pastel-pink showy milkweed (Asclepias speciosa) of British Columbia, Manitoba and California, this species prefers the moist periphery of rivers and swamps. Reaching a height of four feet, this plant may appear individually or in scattered groups. Its range includes Quebec, Ontario, Manitoba and New England south to Texas.

Left:
Small sundrops
(*Oenothera perennis*)

*These tiny, delicate blossoms were found while walking an old dirt road in midsummer. A member of the evening primrose family, this species appears in Quebec, Nova Scotia and Ontario in Canada and in many areas of the United States. One is able to see the structural similarities of the sundrop and the evening primrose (*Oenothera biennis*) in the shape of the stamens and pistils.*

Right:
Queen Anne's lace,
wild carrot (*Daucus carota*)

Belonging to a large family of plants containing about three thousand species, this three-foot summer plant of dry soils is directly related to parsley and celery. In many areas of North America, this species grows in such profusion that it is considered, by some, as a troublesome weed.

Showy lady's slipper
(*Cypripedium reginae*)

The largest of the northern orchids, this spectacular species may reach a height of three feet. Found throughout much of the northeastern United States and north into Newfoundland, Ontario, Manitoba and Saskatchewan, the showy lady's slipper prefers the cool shade of moist woodlands or the periphery of swamps and bogs. In many areas this beautiful orchid is endangered or rare, and protected by law.

Dense blazing star
(*Liatris spicata*)

This strikingly elegant six-foot plant bears a dense cluster of feathery blossoms at its head. A member of the composite family, blazing star may be found in such diverse regions as Florida and southwestern Ontario. Dense blazing star prefers low, moist soils, although related species such as the rough blazing star (Liatris aspere), flourish under much drier conditions.

Small round-leaved orchis
(*Orchis rotundifolia*)

One of the smallest north-
ern orchids, the small round-
leaved orchis is a beautiful
sight in its habitat of lime-
stone swamps and wet
woodlands. The diminutive
cluster of magenta-dappled
blossoms is delicately
perched at the top of a
slender, ten-inch stem. The
plant is considered rare in
many parts of its eastern-
most range.

Left:
Spotted touch-me-not, jewelweed
(*Impatiens capensis*)

Flourishing communal masses of these pendant blossoms may be found in midsummer. Inhabiting cool, shaded shores of ponds and streambanks, this species has a wide range in North America. The delicate, red-spotted orange flowers attract nectar-seeking hummingbirds and butterflies.

Right:
Thread-leaved sundew
(*Drosera filiformis*)

Enormous carpets of this carnivorous plant may be seen from southern Canada and Massachusetts to Florida, as well as in numerous other locales. Other species of sundew, such as the round-leaved sundew (Drosera rotundifolia), grow in similar habitats.

Left:
Day lily
(*Hemerocallis fulva*)

One of many species of flower to be brought to our shores, the day lily is originally from Eurasia. A communal plant, this four-foot lily now appears in clusters throughout much of eastern North America. Each of its large blossoms lasts for only a day.

Right:
Butter and eggs, toadflax
(*Linaria vulgaris*)

This plant's common name offers insight into the immense problem of identifying plants by their common name alone. The butter and eggs (Orthocarpus erianthus) known to Californians is, as its botanical name reveals, a totally different plant.

Wild bergamot (*Monarda fistulosa*)

A member of the mint family, wild bergamot is directly related to catnip (Nepeta cataria) and peppermint (Mentha piperita). Reaching a height of four feet, this lovely plant bears a lilac-colored blossom and can be seen in the dry fields and meadows of eastern Canada and as far south as Alabama and Texas.

Evening primrose
(*Oenothera biennis*)

Found throughout most of northeastern and northcentral North America, this tall, stately plant may reach a height of almost five feet. Appearing from late June to September, these flowers are most often seen scattered along roadsides, abandoned railway lines and the dry soils of open terrain. Each one- to two-inch flower bears a delicate aroma of lemon and produces seeds that provide a valuable source of food for birds.

Moth mullein
(*Verbascum blattaria*)

The fuzzy stamens of the moth mullein resemble the antennae of moths. This plant, like its relative the common mullein (Verbascum thapsus), appears in dry meadows, fields and roadside ditches throughout the United States and southern Canada.

Left: Swamp rose mallow (*Hibiscus palustris*)

A stately plant of summer, this large hibiscus may reach a height of eight feet. Frequenting the coastal salt marshes of Massachusetts south to Florida and some inland freshwater marshes of the lower Great Lakes area, these flowers often reach a width of seven inches. In some areas this species is now regarded as both rare and endangered.

Above: Bladder campion (*Silene cucubalus*)

Originally a species of Eurasia, this flower now inhabits much of southern Canada south to Missouri, Oregon and Colorado. Appearing in clusters in the dry fields and roadsides of summer, it is the veined, translucent and swollen calyx of this one-inch flower that gives the species its common name.

Tall ironweed (*Vernonia altissima*)

A member of the sunflower family, this seven-foot plant is related to both zinnias and dahlias, as well as to lettuce and artichokes. There are approximately 19,000 species of sunflower worldwide.

Above: Devil's paintbrush (*Hieracium aurantiacum*)

Not a true paintbrush (Castilleja sp.), this familiar weed of roadsides and fields was given its common name by exasperated farmers whose pastureland is often ruined by its rapid spread. Its bright orange flowers, nonetheless, make a pretty sight to passers-by.

Right: Nodding bur-marigold (*Bidens cernua*)

As this plant matures, the flower heads begin to droop or "nod." Like its relative, the marsh marigold (Caltha palustris), this plant regularly appears in groups in wet soils and swampy areas. Found throughout most of southern Canada, the nodding bur-marigold also inhabits a wide range in the United States' Pacific region.

Canada thistle (*Cirsium arvense*)

The Canada thistle, originally a European species, was first introduced to this continent in Canada. Today, much of eastern and central North America and parts of the Pacific coast are inhabited by this familiar plant.

Left:
Wild calla, water arum
(*Calla palustris*)

Wild calla is a plant of cool wetlands, bogs and the edges of ponds and can be found throughout much of Canada, Alaska and the eastern and midwestern United States. This particular member of the arum family also inhabits Eurasia, while other family members grow in the tropics. Some, such as the dieffenbachia, have become familiar house plants.

Right:
Prickly rose
(*Rosa acicularis*)

The showy two-inch blossoms of this native species may be found in many dry fields, ditches and open woodland habitats from Alaska to Quebec and south to Colorado in the mountains. Roses have a long history of human use, particularly in the manufacture of perfumes.

Left:
Harebell
(*Campanula rotundifolia*)

This hardy perennial inhabits an enormous range, including the sparse, bitter environment of the arctic shoreline, high mountainous regions and the open woods and meadows of Pennsylvania, Illinois and California. A circumpolar species, it is the famous bluebell of Scotland, and in California is, in fact, known as the Scotch bluebell.

Right:
Common St. John's wort
(*Hypericum perforatum*)

Frequenting dry meadows and grassy knolls, this bright yellow European native now appears throughout an enormous range in North America. Many plants, once foreign to our continent, now grow here in great numbers. Some have caused severe damage to our native environments, altering them forever. Others, like this flower, have been benign additions to our wildflower population.

Above: Common milkweed (*Asclepias syriaca*)

*The interdependence of plants and animals is nowhere more beautifully exhibited than in the relationship between the milkweeds and the migratory monarch butterfly whose caterpillars feed exclusively on the foliage of this family of plants. This leafy species has relatives spread throughout much of North America including the showy milkweed (*Asclepias speciosa*) *and butterfly-weed (*Asclepias tuberosa*).*

Right: Bull thistle (*Cirsium vulgare*)

Reaching a height of six feet, the bull thistle is one of the largest and most common species of thistle. The downy, white filaments attached to the seeds of this plant facilitate their dispersal by the wind. In late summer these same seeds are a valuable food source for the beautiful American goldfinch which also uses the fluffy filaments as a lining for its nest.

Left:
Lance-leaved coreopsis
(*Coreopsis lanceolata*)

Sun-drenched colonies of this two-foot-high sunflower may often be seen at road-sides or in the sandy or rock-strewn soils of Virginia, Florida northward to Michigan, Wisconsin and southern Ontario.

Right.
White bog orchis
(*Platanthera dilatata*)

Found in many cold-water bogs and wet meadows, this elegant spike of fragrant blossoms is one of the most noticeable native orchids. In bloom by midsummer, this stately, candle-like plant appears throughout much of Canada and in favored habitats in Minnesota, Wisconsin and Michigan.

Ox-eye daisy (*Chrysanthemum leucanthemum*)

Introduced to North America from Europe, the ox-eye daisy now appears throughout much of the United States and Canada. Enormous communal masses of this three-foot plant are a common sight in meadows and roadside ditches in summer.

Left:
Sheep laurel
(*Kalmia angustifolia*)

A relative of the showy rho-
dodendrons that flourish in
many gardens, the sheep
laurel is a low, evergreen
shrub that reaches a height
of approximately three feet.
Labrador tea (Ledum groen-
landicum), as well as cran-
berries and blueberries, are
related to this beautiful pink
plant.

Right:
Smooth false foxglove
(*Aureolaria laevigata*)

Hundreds of the yellow blos-
soms of the smooth false
foxglove may appear in the
open woodland and elevat-
ed regions of Ohio, Pennsyl-
vania south to Georgia, and
in other regions offering
similar habitats. This spe-
cies is semi-parasitic and
commonly takes nutrients
from the roots of oak trees.

Left:
Deptford pink
(*Dianthus armeria*)

*Introduced to this continent from Europe, these tiny blossoms may now be found flourishing in many dry fields and roadside ditches over a wide area. Its relatives include the bladder campion (*Silene cucubalus*) and the blood-red blossoms of the California Indian pink (*Silene californica*).*

Right:
Hoary puccoon
(*Lithospermum canescens*)

*Puccoon is an Indian word for plants that yield dyes. Related to the European true forget-me-not (*Myosotis scorpioides*), and to the North American native, the smaller forget-me-not (*Myosotis laxa*), hoary puccoon may be found in dry, sandy soils from Saskatchewan and Ontario south to Texas.*

Moccasin flower, pink lady's slipper
(*Cypripedium acaule*)

One of the larger native orchids, this beautifully-veined blossom may be found throughout eastern North America. In late spring and early summer, many coniferous and mixed forests harbor large numbers of this fragile plant.

Moccasin flower (rare white form)
(*Cypripedium acaule*)

Although the moccasin flower, or pink lady's slipper, is almost always a delicate, veined pink, it appears occasionally as an all-white bloom.

Rough-fruited cinquefoil (*Potentilla recta*)

Native to Europe, this common two-foot-high plant of midsummer now inhabits a large area of North America. Prolific and well-adapted to dry fields and roadsides, it is regarded by many as an obnoxious weed.

Left:
Teasel
(*Dipsacus sylvestris*)

*Large masses of this spikey six-foot plant may be seen in late summer. Originally a European native, it is now well-established in North America, frequenting the waste soils and ditches of British Columbia, California, Ontario and Quebec. A relative, Fuller's teasel (*Dipsacus fullonum*), appears in the Pacific states region.*

Right:
Tall meadow-rue
(*Thalictrum polygamum*)

*Tall, billowing masses of this eight-foot plant are a common sight of summer. Inhabiting the moist meadows and the periphery of swamps and rivers from Ontario, Quebec and Nova Scotia to New England and beyond, this species is favored by many butterflies and other flying insects. A member of the buttercup family, it is related to the marsh marigold (*Caltha palustris*).*

Left:
Yellow iris
(*Iris pseudacorus*)

A European native species, this three-foot plant was brought to North America for garden use. It has since spread to favorable natural habitats throughout much of the northeastern United States and southern portions of Canada. A native yellow iris, the golden iris (Iris innominata), may be found in southwest Oregon.

Right:
Purple loosestrife
(*Lythrum salicaria*)

Introduced from Europe, this aggressive, communal and showy perennial often appears in spectacular fields of solid magenta. Flowering profusely in many marshes and moist meadows throughout the eastern region of North America, this plant may also be found in Australia and North Africa.

One-flowered cancer root,
naked broomrape
(*Orobanche uniflora*)

*An inhabitant of cool, moist
thickets, this leafless, parasitic plant obtains its nutrients from the roots of other
plants. Found throughout
much of North America from
Alaska and Quebec to California and Florida, the white
plant of the eastern range is
supplanted by a mauve
flower in the west.*

Fireweed
(*Epilobium angustifolium*)

A member of the evening primrose family of plants, this showy, communal native flower is one of the very first to appear in the wake of a forest fire, hence its name. Tall and elegant, individual plants may reach a height of six feet and the bright pink flowers are a familiar sight in fields, roadsides and burnt-over ground across North America.

Yellow loosestrife,
swamp candles
(*Lysimachia terrestris*)

*Elegant, candle-like forms
standing in a swamp sig-
nal the presence of this three-
foot native plant. This species belongs to the primrose
family, while the European
native purple loosestrife
(*Lythrum salicaria*) belongs
to the loosestrife family.*

Flower Photography

After its invention in 1839, photography began to offer new, startling insights into the world about us. In Europe in the 1860s, portrait painters barely survived the onslaught of this new visual medium. Within a brief twenty years, Edward Muybridge had frozen in time his sequential images of galloping horses, and by 1885 George Eastman had invented the first Kodak box camera. Many years and optical inventions later, we can now travel to distant lands or into our own backyards to photograph the beautiful wildflowers found growing there. Rather than disturbing the flowers, we are able, through the use of the camera, to enjoy our outings, returning home not with blossoms that soon whither and die, but instead with beautiful images to share with friends for many years to come.

Wildflower photography, and nature photography in general, offers us many challenges and as many rewards. Successful photographs often depend upon a variety of things. Invariably, fickle weather, pesky insects and faulty alarm clocks must be contended with, as well as goocy bogs, jammed film cassettes and flat tires. Despite such things, nature photography becomes, for many people, a lifelong exploration into the habits, the domains and life cycles of earth's living treasures.

Many dozens of photographic technique books proliferate and many of these appear to offer quick, simple shortcuts to the mastery of film and the idiosyncracies of cameras. Yet, from my experience, the challenge before us all is one of perception, one of learning how best to observe and render on film the delicacies of natural light, the fragile and eloquent beauty of the living things about us. Hopefully, the images in this book will encourage you to begin your own explorations of the natural habitats nearest you. Hopefully, too, you will take your camera and notebooks, field guides and insect-repellent with you, to begin to record, in your own fashion, the floral world about you.

Invariably, I am asked how best to begin, with what equipment and at what expense. Wild-flower photography does not require enormous amounts of money or tremendously expensive equipment. Except for environmental photographs, which can be executed well with standard lenses, many photographs of tiny flowers, or details of flowers, however, do require the ability to focus at very close range. Most standard lenses restrict such close focusing of subjects. My 85 mm portrait lens, as an example, only allows me to work at a minimum focus distance to the subject of three feet. At this distance, many flowers occupy only a small portion of the film area. Ultimately, however, my camera may only be inches from the blossom being photographed. To achieve such close subject-to-film distances, a number of equipment options are available, the most expensive of which are macro lenses. Although I use a 100 mm macro lens for much of my close-up work, manual or automatic bellows are noticeably less expensive than the average macro lens and most major camera manufacturers produce them for the marketplace. What is of great benefit in the purchase of a bellows is that, in most instances, differing focal-length lenses (from the standard 50 mm lens to medium and even long telephoto lenses) may be used with it. Accordingly, the fixed minimum focus range of any lens can be radically altered, allowing for much closer focusing of the subject.

Perhaps the single most valuable and important piece of equipment for wildflower photography is a solid, versatile tripod that allows the camera to be placed a fraction of an inch from the ground. Any movement of the camera or the flower during an exposure on film produces a blurred photograph. Slow film such as Kodachrome 25 ISO demands a long exposure time and many of the photographs in this book required two or more seconds of exposure. A hand-held camera is a useless tool for photographing hepatica on a cold spring morning when attached to a shivering photographer.

Most of the photographs in this book were done with 35 mm single-lens reflex cameras using only Kodachrome 25 and 64 ISO film. A few, such as the prickly pear cactus and the trumpet creeper, were photographed using a medium-format 6 × 7 camera and Ektachrome 64 ISO

film. A tripod and cable release were used in every case.

The purchase of one or more wildflower identification field guides will certainly help you, particularly if your knowledge of native wildflowers is as limited as mine was ten years ago. Researching your subjects before they blossom really helps to give some ideas as to where and when best to begin searching for the particular species of interest. A number of excellent reference books and field guides have been listed in this book for your use. Many more fine publications exist.

An avid, amateur botanist and friend once gave me verbal directions to the location of a beautiful yellow lady's slipper orchid. Eventually, I found the orchid but the group wasn't the one for which I received the directions. For this reason I suggest that you keep a notebook on your journeys. As you explore each area, such a book will allow you to record the names, flowering dates and locations of many plants for future reference. It will become your own field guide.

Meeting other people who share the same enthusiasm for the outdoors is one of the most enjoyable aspects of exploring nature with a camera. Although much of my work involves traveling and camping alone, I am sometimes joined by good friends with whom I may spend a day of hiking and photography. Fellow bird-watchers and nature photographers are generally a gregarious lot and many long sunset hours have been spent about a campsite sharing ideas and stories. Much of what I have learned about photography, and about plants and animals, is the result of such warm camaraderie. Much of what you will learn, too, as you step out into nature's realm with your camera, will be the result of sharing your experiences with others.

As you get more involved, you will discover that photographing plants and animals will often mean groping around on hands and knees to see them from new perspectives, in new lights and with new meaning. Because of this, the camera and weather-beaten jeans seem to go hand in hand and the results of your experiences will often be soiled elbows and bemused or inquisitive passers-by. But, as well, nature photography will give you many memories of time spent with good friends in beautiful places. Whether you seek an avocation or a professional status with a camera, I believe nature photography can become a lifelong voyage of discovery.

Reading List

Ferguson, M. and R.M. Saunders. *Canadian Wildflowers*. Toronto: Van Nostrand Reinhold Ltd., 1976.

Ferguson, M. and R.M. Saunders. *Canadian Wildflowers through the Seasons*. Toronto: Van Nostrand Reinhold Ltd., 1982.

Newcomb, Lawrence and R.C. Clement. *Newcomb's Wildflower Guide*. Boston: Little, Brown and Company, 1977.

Niehaus, Theodore F. and Charles L. Ripper. *A Field Guide to Pacific States Wildflowers*. Boston: Houghton Mifflin, Co., 1976.

Niering, W.A. and N.C. Olmstead. *The Audubon Society Field Guide to North American Wildflowers: Eastern Region*. New York: Alfred A. Knopf Inc., 1979.

Peterson, Roger Tory. *A Field Guide to the Birds: Eastern Region*. Boston: Houghton Mifflin, Co., 1980.

Peterson, Roger Tory and Margaret McKenny. *A Field Guide to Wildflowers: Northeastern and Northcentral North America*. Boston: Houghton Mifflin, Co., 1968.

Petrie, William. *Guide to Orchids of North America*. North Vancouver: Hancock House Publishers Ltd., 1981.

Pyle, R.M. *The Audubon Society Field Guide to North American Butterflies*. New York: Alfred A. Knopf Inc., 1981.

Williams, John G. and Andrew E. Williams. *Field Guide to Orchids of North America*. New York: Universe Books, 1983.

Photo Index